ALTERNATOR
BOOKS™

INCREDIBLE SPORTS TRIVIA

FUN FACTS AND QUIZZES

Eric Braun

Lerner Publications ◆ Minneapolis

Lerner Publications Company
A division of Lerner Publishing Group, Inc.
241 First Avenue North
Minneapolis, MN 55401 USA

For reading levels and more information, look up this title at
www.lernerbooks.com.

Main body text set in Aptifer Slab LT Pro Regular.
Typeface provided by Linotype AG.

Library of Congress Cataloging-in-Publication Data

Names: Braun, Eric, 1971– author.
Title: Incredible sports trivia : fun facts and quizzes / Eric Braun.
Description: Minneapolis : Lerner Publications, 2018. | Series: Trivia
    Time! | Includes bibliographical references. | Audience: Age 8–12. |
    Audience: Grade 4 to 6.
Identifiers: LCCN 2017010791 (print) | LCCN 2017015562 (ebook) |
    ISBN 9781512483383 (eb pdf) | ISBN 9781512483338 (lb : alk. paper)
Subjects: LCSH: Sports—Miscellanea—Juvenile literature.
Classification: LCC GV707 (ebook) | LCC GV707 .B72 2018 (print) |
    DDC 796—dc23

LC record available at https://lccn.loc.gov/2017010791

Manufactured in the United States of America
1-43340-33160-8/3/2017

CONTENTS

SOCCER

The Super Bowl is the most popular sporting event in the United States. More than 111 million people watched it on TV in 2017. But worldwide, it is not even close to the most popular. More than one *billion* people watched the final game of soccer's 2014 FIFA World Cup in Brazil!

Believe it or not, early soccer players used the inflated bladders of livestock as their soccer balls!

Q. The first FIFA World Cup was held in 1930. When did the first FIFA Women's World Cup take place?

A. November 1991, 61 years after the first men's FIFA World Cup teams played. The FIFA Women's World Cup has been going strong every four years since that groundbreaking game, in which the US team scored its way to victory.

Mind Blown: Real Madrid star Cristiano Ronaldo's legs are insured for 140 million euros. That's about $148 million. Can you even imagine that kind of money!?

The lights at the 2014 FIFA World Cup in Brazil were so bright that US astronaut Reid Wiseman was able to take some pretty clear photos of the stadiums—from outer space!

Soccer great Pelé scored an incredible 1,281 goals in his professional career. In 2000 he was named FIFA Player of the Century, along with Argentina's Diego Maradona.

OLYMPIC SPORTS

American swimmer Michael Phelps has won more gold medals than any other Olympic athlete in history. This star of the pool has brought home an astounding 23 golds. That's more gold medals than most entire countries have won.

Q. Can you guess how many events took place at the first recorded Olympic Games in 776 BCE?

A. Just one. It was a 192-meter footrace, won by a man named Coroebus.

Q. In what Olympic sport do athletes perform the following moves: toe jumps, edge jumps, upright spins, sit spins, steps, turns, spirals, and lifts?

A. Figure skating

Q. What is a hippodrome?

A. A tricky high-diving technique
B. An ancient stadium for horse racing
C. A special kind of track used in early Olympic running competitions
D. A feeding pen for large mammals

A. If you guessed B, you're correct. It's an oval-shaped stadium where horse and chariot races took place in ancient Greece.

American Simone Biles won a remarkable four gold medals in artistic gymnastics in 2016. It was the most ever for an American in her sport!

Jamaican sprinter Usain Bolt is the world's fastest human. At the 2008 Olympics in Beijing, China, he won the gold and set the world record in the 100-meter dash. He successfully defended his title at the 2012 and 2016 Olympics too, winning gold both times.

Richard Norris Williams won gold in mixed doubles tennis at the 1924 Olympic Games in Paris, France—12 years after nearly dying aboard the *Titanic*.

BASEBALL

Baseball is said to have been invented by Abner Doubleday in Cooperstown, New York, around 1840. This story has persisted into the modern day, but there's one problem: it isn't true! Early forms of baseball were played in what is now the United States long before the 1800s. Immigrants probably brought versions of the game from their home countries.

After the Chicago Cubs won the World Series in 2016, the Cleveland Indians became the team with the longest title drought in Major League Baseball. They haven't won a championship since 1948.

Q. In 2006 Detroit Tigers pitcher Joel Zumaya missed the American League Championship Series due to an injury. Can you guess what the injury was?

A. He strained his wrist playing the video game *Guitar Hero.*

In 1859 a sportswriter named Henry Chadwick invented this.

  A. The box score

  B. The phrase *home run*

  C. The phrase *suicide squeeze*

  D. The seventh-inning stretch

The answer is A. In Chadwick's time, games weren't captured through photography, let alone on television or the Internet. Chadwick's box scores helped fans follow baseball games.

Q. Do you know who holds the record for throwing the fastest fastball?

A. It's Cuban reliever Aroldis Chapman. His fastball has been clocked at an amazing 105.1 miles (169.1 km) per hour.

Q. What hitter has won the most MLB batting titles?

A. It's Ty Cobb. No wonder he's considered one of the greatest baseball players of all time.

The New York Yankees have 27 World Series titles, more than any other team. The second-best team is way behind, with 11. Which team is it?

A. The Boston Red Sox
B. The New York Giants
C. The Philadelphia Athletics
D. The St. Louis Cardinals

It's D, the St. Louis Cardinals—but 11 wins is still pretty impressive!

FAMOUS FIRSTS

First professional baseball pitcher to throw a curveball:

William Arthur "Candy" Cummings

First women's college basketball game:

Stanford vs. the University of California in 1896 (Stanford won)

First golfer to hit a hole-in-one:

Young Tom Morris

First-ever volleyball game:

1895 at the Holyoke, Massachusetts, YMCA

First indoor football game:

December 28, 1902, between the New York Knickerbockers and the Syracuse Athletic Club

Football's first forward pass:

1906, when St. Louis University's Bradbury Robinson threw 20 yards to Jack Schneider in a game against Carroll College in Waukesha, Wisconsin

Basketball's first slam dunk:

1936, when American Joe Fortenberry jumped into the air and shoved the ball down through the basket at the Olympics

TENNIS

The four most important pro tennis tournaments are called Grand Slam events. Which of the following is *not* a Grand Slam?

A. Wimbledon
B. Ryder Cup
C. US Open
D. Australian Open

B, the Ryder Cup. That one's a golf competition. The fourth Grand Slam event is the French Open.

Wimbledon players must dress almost from head to toe in white. The rule probably started in the 1800s, because people didn't want to see the sweaty spots that can sometimes appear on colored clothes.

Q. The word *tennis* comes from the French word *tenez*. What does that word mean?

A. "I am ready to serve!" Players in 13th-century France said this word when serving.

Australian Margaret Court has won the most Grand Slam singles titles of any player in history, with 24. But Serena Williams is right on her heels, with 23. Court also holds the record for most Grand Slam titles overall, with 62.

When was the first Wimbledon tournament?

A. 1900
B. 1952
C. 1877
D. 1918

The answer is C, 1877. Yes, Wimbledon really is that old!

On May 9, 2012, Australian Samuel Groth hit the fastest recorded tennis serve. It went 163.4 miles (263 km) per hour. Unfortunately for Groth, the blazing serve was not enough to get him the win—he lost 6–4, 6–3.

Q. What is it called when a player wins the singles, doubles, and mixed doubles at all four Grand Slams?

A. A boxed set

GOLF

The modern version of golf is believed to have been invented in Scotland. Yet in 1457, James II, the king of Scotland, passed a law banning the sport. He said golf was interfering too much with archery practice, which he thought was important for national defense.

Golf was played at the Olympics for the first time in Paris in 1900.

One of the greatest athletes of all time was Babe Didrikson Zaharias, a golfer who also excelled in basketball and track and field. Can you guess how many golf tournaments she won?

A. 15

B. 36

C. 55

D. 82

Amazingly, the answer is D. And Zaharias won 14 of those 82 tournaments in a row!

In 1900 a new golf ball was introduced that was made with a rubber core. Golf balls before this had been made with gutta-percha, a plastic-like substance from sapodilla trees. The rubber-core balls were much cheaper than the earlier balls, so the popularity of golf exploded!

In February 1971, *Apollo 14* astronaut Alan Shepard became the first person to hit a golf ball on the moon when he smacked two balls with a six iron.

American golfer Ab Smith was playing a round in the late 1800s when he hit a really excellent shot. He called his shot a bird—a term that in his time referred to something amazing. Smith went on to complete the hole at one under par (which is very good in golf), and soon everyone was calling a score of one under par a birdie!

The Toonik Tyme Festival in Iqaluit, Nunavut, Canada, features a nine-hole snow golf course. Players use fluorescent balls because white balls would get lost in the snow!

Do you know which golfer has won the most major championships in men's golf?

A. Arnold Palmer
B. Tiger Woods
C. Gary Player
D. Jack Nicklaus

If you picked D, you got it. Nicklaus has won 18 majors.

MOTOR-SPORTS

The brake discs on a Formula 1 car have to withstand an operating temperature of about 1,832°F (1,000°C). They are made of carbon fiber. It is much harder than steel and has a higher melting point.

Q. Richard Petty is known as the king of stock car racing. He has the most wins of any racer. How many wins do you think he has?

A. He has 200 wins. He definitely is the king!

Q. Who is the oldest living Formula 1 driver?

A. Stirling Moss, who was born on September 17, 1929. Moss took the checkered flag 16 times between 1951 and 1961.

When Trevor Bayne won the Daytona 500 in 2011, he became the youngest driver to do so. He was 20 years old. In 1988 Bobby Allison won it at the age of 50, making him the oldest.

Three father-son duos have won the Daytona 500. Which of the following pairs has *not* done it?

A. Lee and Richard Petty
B. Dale Earnhardt Jr. and Sr.
C. Mario and Michael Andretti
D. Bobby and Davey Allison

It's C, Mario and Michael Andretti. Surprised? The Andrettis may be one of the most famous racing families of all time, but only Mario has won the Daytona 500.

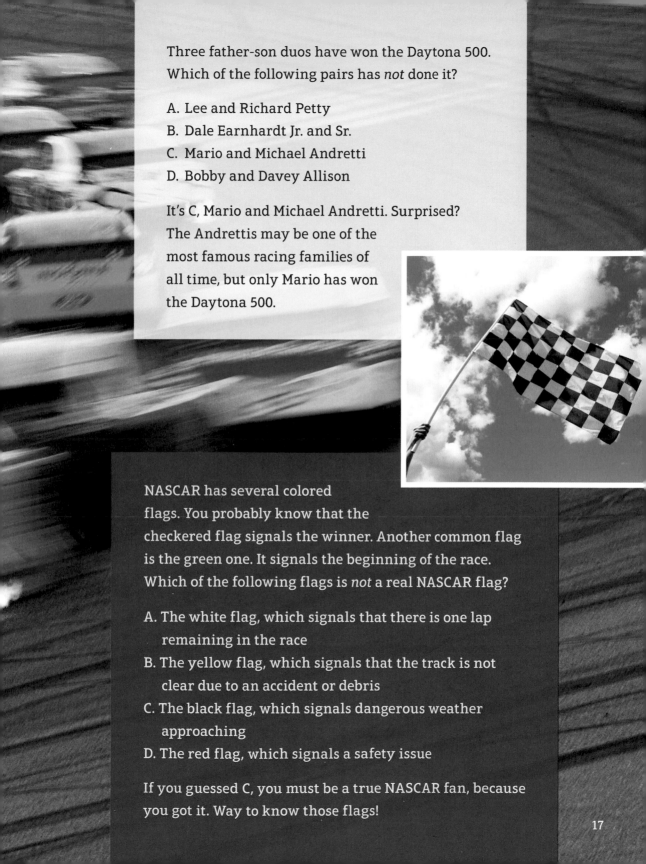

NASCAR has several colored flags. You probably know that the checkered flag signals the winner. Another common flag is the green one. It signals the beginning of the race. Which of the following flags is *not* a real NASCAR flag?

A. The white flag, which signals that there is one lap remaining in the race
B. The yellow flag, which signals that the track is not clear due to an accident or debris
C. The black flag, which signals dangerous weather approaching
D. The red flag, which signals a safety issue

If you guessed C, you must be a true NASCAR fan, because you got it. Way to know those flags!

FOOTBALL

This player is the career leader in rushing yards, with 18,355.

A. Jim Brown

C. Adrian Peterson

B. Walter Payton

D. Emmitt Smith

It's D, Emmitt Smith, running back for the Dallas Cowboys and Arizona Cardinals in the 1990s and early 2000s.

Mind Blown: Seattle Seahawks fans cheered so loudly in a January 2014 playoff game against the New Orleans Saints that they caused an earthquake! And it's not even the only earthquake Seahawks fans have brought on. They also caused a quake with their cheering in 2011— in another playoff game against the Saints.

Former Minnesota Vikings kicker Fred Cox was also an inventor. What did he invent?

A. The Nerf football
B. The Diaper Genie
C. The modern football helmet
D. The FaceCradle Travel Pillow

The answer is A, the Nerf football— and who better than a pro football player to design the ball that introduces many kids to the sport?

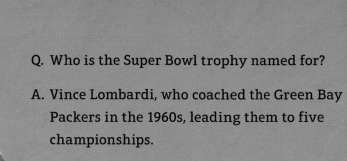

Q. Who is the Super Bowl trophy named for?

A. Vince Lombardi, who coached the Green Bay Packers in the 1960s, leading them to five championships.

Q. An average NFL game lasts more than three hours. But how much of that is actual live football action?

A. Just 11 minutes. That means football fans who catch the sport on TV spend almost three full hours watching commercials, replays, challenges, and shots of players standing around.

Jerry Rice has played in four Super Bowls and caught eight touchdowns in the big game—more than any other player in history!

Football's history is filled with great nicknames, like Sweetness for Walter Payton and Ed "Too Tall" Jones. Which of the following was *not* a real player's nickname?

A. William "the Refrigerator" Perry
B. Larry "the Cable Guy" Csonka
C. Mean Joe Greene
D. Broadway Joe Namath

The answer is B. There is no Cable Guy in football!

FLUBS, FAILS, AND MAJOR MESS-UPS

Using his head: Jose Canseco of the Texas Rangers once let a ball bounce off the top of his head and over the fence for a home run.

Leaps and bounds: In an Olympic basketball game, France's Frédéric Weis tried to block American Vince Carter from making a shot. What he didn't count on was his opponent's jumping skills. Carter leaped right over Weis's head to dunk the ball—and even more amazing? Weis is more than 7 feet (2.1 m) tall!

Bad trade: In 1989 Minnesota Vikings general manager Mike Lynn traded five players as well as several draft picks to the Dallas Cowboys for running back Hershel Walker (*above*). The Vikings won zero playoff games with Walker. But with the picks the Cowboys got in the deal, they won three of the next four Super Bowls!

Really bad trade: In 1919 the Boston Red Sox traded one of their players to the New York Yankees for cash. The player? Babe Ruth (*right*). In the 15 years after the trade—the rest of Ruth's career—Boston never finished higher than fourth place. The Yankees won four World Series during that time, thanks largely to Ruth's talent.

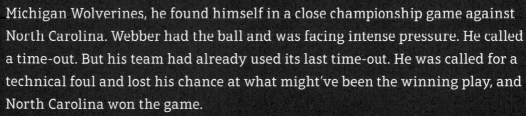

Unfortunate call: When NBA star Chris Webber was in college playing for the Michigan Wolverines, he found himself in a close championship game against North Carolina. Webber had the ball and was facing intense pressure. He called a time-out. But his team had already used its last time-out. He was called for a technical foul and lost his chance at what might've been the winning play, and North Carolina won the game.

Midair blunder: American snowboarder Lindsey Jacobellis (*below*) had a solid lead in the women's snowboardcross event at the 2006 Olympics in Turin, Italy. She decided to add some flair to one of the jumps. She did a fancy grab called a method air—but she held the grab too long and fell. She tumbled across the snow, and her chance of winning gold tumbled away as well.

Epic miss: In Game 6 of the 1986 World Series, Mookie Wilson of the New York Mets hit a slow ground ball toward first base. It should have been an easy play for Boston Red Sox first baseman Bill Buckner. But Buckner missed the ball, and it rolled between his legs. The Mets went on to score, giving them the win. This tied the Series, which the Red Sox lost in Game 7.

BASKETBALL

Q. James Naismith invented basketball in 1891 as a way to entertain a group of boys in a gym. He used a soccer ball for the ball. What did he use for the basket?

A. A peach basket

The average NBA player is 6 feet 7 (2 m). But the two tallest players in NBA history were Manute Bol and Gheorghe Muresan, who were both 7 feet 7 (2.3 m)!

Kareem Abdul-Jabbar holds the record for most points scored in a career. How many points do you think he scored?

A. 38,387
B. 25,046
C. 31,042
D. 29,736

Incredibly, the answer is A, which is why Abdul-Jabbar is considered one of the best basketball players to ever take to the court.

Tina Thompson is the career WNBA points leader. How many points has she scored?

A. 6,262
B. 6,312
C. 7,488
D. 6,998

It's C. No wonder Thompson is a legend in her sport!

The shortest player in NBA history was Muggsy Bogues, who's just 5 feet 3 (1.6 m). The point guard made up for his lack of stature with great vision, quick hands, and outstanding defense skills.

UCLA is known as one of the nation's best schools for basketball fans. Its men's team has won 11 NCAA titles, including a run of seven titles in a row from 1967 to 1973.

The University of Connecticut women's team has won 11 national titles as well—plus 43 conference titles! It's another great school for those who love to see talent on the court.

What was the Carrier Classic?

A. A college basketball game played on an aircraft carrier
B. The signature pump fake move of point guard Mark Carrier
C. A once-popular play in which a player would leap from beyond the free throw line and complete a slam dunk
D. A game played just for fun in which two college basketball teams played each other while carrying teammates on their shoulders

The answer is A—and while the Carrier Classic no longer exists, an aircraft carrier *was* a pretty cool place to host a game of hoops.

HOCKEY

When the NHL first started in 1917, it had just five teams: the Montreal Canadiens, the Montreal Wanderers, the Toronto Arenas, the Ottawa Senators, and the Quebec Bulldogs.

Q. Who has scored the most points in NHL history?

A. Wayne Gretzky, with 2,857, and it's not even close. Jaromir Jagr is in second place with 1,909.

Wayne Gretzky was so dominant, he holds many other records as well, including netting 50 of these.

A. Player of the Week Awards
B. ESPN Golden Skates Awards
C. Hat tricks
D. Product endorsements

The answer is C, hat tricks—or the scoring of three goals in one game by a single player.

In the late 1800s, the Montreal Amateur Athletic Association became the first team to ever win the Stanley Cup—the highest honor in the sport of hockey and the oldest trophy competed for by pro athletes in North America.

Today we call it a face-off. What was the first play in hockey called in the original rules?

A. A clash
B. A stick-bash
C. A charge
D. A bully

If you guessed D, you're right. In early hockey games, the word *bully* **didn't refer to a player who pushed other players around—it was simply the name for the game's first play.**

In the early days of hockey, what were pucks made of?

A. Cow dung
B. Pigskin
C. Ice dyed black
D. Coal

Believe it or not, the answer is A. When it came to getting hit with a puck back then, the gross-out factor may have been even higher than the ouch factor.

EXTREME SPORTS AND WEIRD SPORTS

Give them just 10 minutes and competitive eaters can eat a lot. Which of the following *wasn't* consumed in 10 minutes as part of an eating competition?

A. 41 lobster rolls
B. 118 jalapeno poppers
C. 381 saltine crackers
D. 36 peanut butter and banana sandwiches

The answer is C—although the winners might have needed some saltines to help settle their stomachs after winning those competitions.

Fun-loving sports fans in Austin, Texas, invented a game called unicycle football. It is just what it sounds like: football played on unicycles.

Legendary skateboarder Tony Hawk holds the record for most spins midair. At the 1999 X Games, he pulled off a 900. He spun 900 degrees, or two and a half times, after launching off the top of a half-pipe—something no one else had done before in competition.

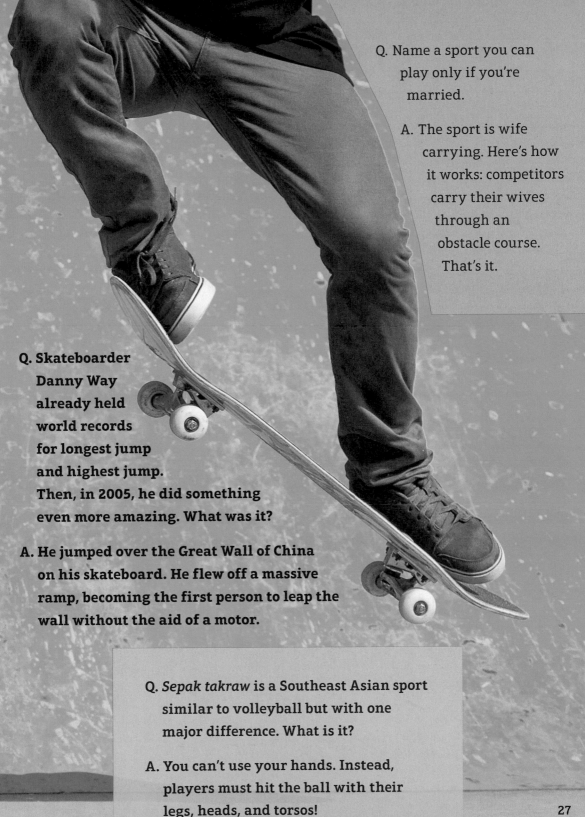

Q. Name a sport you can play only if you're married.

A. The sport is wife carrying. Here's how it works: competitors carry their wives through an obstacle course. That's it.

Q. Skateboarder Danny Way already held world records for longest jump and highest jump. Then, in 2005, he did something even more amazing. What was it?

A. He jumped over the Great Wall of China on his skateboard. He flew off a massive ramp, becoming the first person to leap the wall without the aid of a motor.

Q. *Sepak takraw* is a Southeast Asian sport similar to volleyball but with one major difference. What is it?

A. You can't use your hands. Instead, players must hit the ball with their legs, heads, and torsos!

27

TRUE OR FALSE

Now that you've learned some incredible sports trivia, here's a bonus round. Guess whether each piece of trivia below is true or false, and check the bottom of page 29 for the answers.

1. NBA legend Wilt Chamberlain once scored 100 points in a single game.

2. In 1988 tennis great Steffi Graf won the Australian Open, French Open, US Open, Wimbledon, and the Olympic gold medal—all in the same year. This feat is called the Golden Racket.

3. In crew, or rowing, the athletes face backward.

4. Holy whiplash! A Formula 1 car can accelerate from 0 to about 99.4 miles (160 km) per hour and decelerate back to 0—in just two seconds.

5. Brothers and MLB pitchers Phil Niekro and Joe Niekro won a combined 539 games—and both were knuckleballers, or pitchers who threw in an unusual way that causes the ball to have no spin, making them noteworthy on two counts.

6. The Detroit Lions have not beaten the Green Bay Packers in Green Bay since 1991.

7. The Connecticut Huskies women's basketball team defeated Mississippi State in the Sweet 16 of the 2016 NCAA tournament by a margin of 60 points.

8. Kelly Sildaru became the youngest Winter X Games gold medalist ever when she won the ski slopestyle gold in 2016.

9. Sisters Venus and Serena Williams have 30 Grand Slam singles titles between them, but the two have never faced each other in a Grand Slam final.

1) True. 2) False. It's called a Golden Slam. 3) True. 4) False. But it *can* accelerate that fast in four seconds. 5) True. 6) False. Detroit finally broke that streak in 2015. 7) True. 8) True. She was 13. 9) False. The sisters have duked it out on the court in nine Grand Slam finals—and they remain on good terms!

WHO KNEW!?

Can't get enough trivia? Then you'll love these facts about trivia, knowledge, and the human brain.

- January 4 is National Trivia Day in the United States.

- The trivia game show *Jeopardy!* was originally going to be called *What's the Question?*

- Your brain accounts for about 2 percent of your body weight. But your brain uses 20 percent of your body's oxygen supply and about 20 percent of your body's energy.

- The brain processes pain felt in our bodies, but the brain itself cannot feel pain.

- In January 2016, an 11-year-old girl became one of the youngest people to get a perfect score of 162 on an IQ test, putting her two points higher than genius scientists Stephen Hawking and Albert Einstein.

FURTHER INFORMATION

Buckley, James, Jr. *Scholastic Year in Sports 2017*. New York: Scholastic, 2016.

ESPN
http://www.espn.com

National Geographic. *Quiz Whiz 6: 1,000 Super Fun Mind-Bending Totally Awesome Trivia Questions*. Washington, DC: National Geographic, 2015.

National Geographic. *Weird but True Sports: 300 Wacky Facts about Awesome Athletics*. Washington, DC: National Geographic, 2016.

Savage, Jeff. *Football Super Stats*. Minneapolis: Lerner Publications, 2018.

Schwartz, Heather E. *Incredible Tech Trivia: Fun Facts and Quizzes*. Minneapolis: Lerner Publications, 2018.

Sports Illustrated Kids
https://www.sikids.com

PHOTO ACKNOWLEDGMENTS

The images in this book are used with the permission of: EFKS/ Shutterstock.com, pp. 4–5 (background), 5 (top right); NikolayN/ Shutterstock.com, p. 4 (center right); Eugene Onischenko/ Shutterstock.com, pp. 5 (top left), 9 (top left); artist/Shutterstock. com, pp. 6–7 (background); Paolo Bona/Shutterstock.com, p. 6 (bottom); lazyllama/Shutterstock.com, p. 6 (top); Suzanne Tucker/ Shutterstock.com, p. 7 (top); cunaplus/Shutterstock.com, p. 7 (bottom); iStock.com/33ft, pp. 8–9 (background); iStock.com/Rinek, p. 9 (top right); Dan Thornberg/Shutterstock.com, p. 10 (top); Keattikorn/ Shutterstock.com, pp. 10 (bottom), 14–15 (center); Lightspring/ Shutterstock.com, pp. 11 (top left), 11 (bottom), 22 (bottom); bestv/ Shutterstock.com, p. 11 (top right); iStock.com/Alija, pp. 12–13 (background); iStock.com/stockcam, p. 12 (bottom); iStock.com/ Cybernesco, p. 13 (bottom right); antpkr/Shutterstock.com, pp. 14–15 (bottom); Action Sports Photography/Shutterstock.com, p. 16 (left); Doug James/Shutterstock.com, pp. 16–17 (background); iStock.com/ Niyazz, p. 17 (right); iStock.com/TRITOOTH, pp. 18–19 (center); iStock. com/Yobro10, p. 18 (bottom right); Focus On Sport/Getty Images Sport/Getty Images, p. 20 (right); PhotogIrwin, La Broad, & Pudlin/ Wikimedia Commons (public domain), p. 21 (top); mountainpix/ Shutterstock.com, p. 21 (bottom); iStock.com/mipan, p. 23 (top); iStock.com/Dmytro Aksonov, pp. 24–25 (background), 25 (bottom); pio3/Shutterstock.com, pp. 26–27 (background). Design elements: R-studio/Shutterstock.com; balabolka/Shutterstock.com.

Front cover: © Stephanie Swartz/REX/Shutterstock (basketball); © Yuriy Ponomarev/REX/Shutterstock (flag); © Longchalerm Rungruang/REX/Shutterstock (hockey); winui/Shutterstock.com (tactics); graphixmania/Shutterstock.com (equipment doodles).

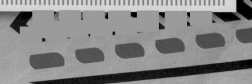